Railway Poetry

Railway Poetry

presented by Zolani Mkiva

Poet of the Nation

FlameTree Media

Published by Flame Tree Media
an imprint of University of Natal Press
Private Bag X01, Scottsville 3209
South Africa

ISBN: 0 86980 989 X

Most of the poems in this volume were first published by SA Railways in *The Railway Magazine* during the late 19th and early 20th century.

Photograph on front cover by AW Smith
Cover design by Lesley Lewis
Layout by Lesley Lewis, Inkspots, Durban
Printed by The Natal Witness, Pietermaritzburg

Printed by Natal Witness Commercial Printers (Pty) Ltd
Pietermaritzburg
9419

In salutation of Transnet Leadership

*Saki Macozoma (Transnet Managing Director),
Louise Tager (Chairperson of Transnet) and
Mafika Mkwanazi (Transnet Managing Director designate)*

Acknowledgements — Zolani Mkiva

From the bottom of my heart, allow me to speak my mind. What comes from my mind and goes through my heart? Naturally I have the impulse of traditional intellect, but allow me to exercise a high sense of corporate discipline and make use of emotional intelligence in addressing you.

"One tree does not make a forest. Right around the sacred tree which we treasure so much, you need to have a myriad of trees to protect and grow it."

I have personally spearheaded the Railway Poetry Project, but there are people I have worked with right from its inception. You will agree with me that any project developed within the ambit of transformation and restructuring is the most challenging one. Indeed we initiated this Railway Poetry Project during the new beginning of Transnet: Transformation and Restructuring was inaugurated within the ranks of our organisation.

Railway poetry has been written from the beginning of time by people from all walks of life. Spoornet has always been proud to keep the material of these writings in its archives. We had to dig down through the old copies of *Railway Magazine* to unearth it. However, one cannot turn a blind eye to the fact that some of the African oral/traditional material was never recorded and therefore could not be part of this project.

But I am glad that at the end of the day we can raise our fists and shout: Railway Poetry.

Let me recognise the Department of Corporate Communication for their willingness and commitment to transformation by allowing me to pursue this Railway Poetry Project. To the head of the Department Dr VVO Mkhize: I would like to thank you for having faith in me. To my immediate Line Manager, Mr Ephraim Mohale (Senior Manager – Corporate Positioning): Thank you for motivating me and allowing me to grow.

I would like to single out Mr Mabila Mathebula (Manager – Rail Safety) who has been my right hand man in this project. It was Mabila together with me who introduced the concept of "Industrial Poetry" which was meant to assist in communicating the message of trans-formation by applying user-friendly mental modes of globalisation.

It would be a serious omission on my part if I did not acknowledge the effort and devotion of Eric Conradie (Railway Historian) in this project.

I would also like to pay special thanks to the following people: Robert Magwaza (Spoornet Official Photographer), Ntokozo Gwamanda, Ocean Mokobane, Nomsa Khanyile, Mandisa Kalako-Williams, Eldene Windvogel, Khaya Mama, Martha Mathiba, Nolwandle Magona, Johan Hugo, Kwezi Kwake, Faith Mtyida, Zetu Mazolwana, Mabila Mathbula, Chain Vilakazi, Nelisa Khumalo, Clive Mavumbe, Nomawethu Duruwe, Moses Skosana, Onele Ludidi, Gina Chauke, Joel Maja, Kathy Jaftha, Prince Xhanti Sigcawu, Paul Leisegang, Tashline Jooste, Johan Vollenhofen, Dimo Mkiva, Voti Zatu, Katrien de Beer, Antoinette Anthony, Hector Dambuza, Sibongile Mkiva, Joseph Jackson, Johan Roodt, Ragmah Jappie, Ringo Madlingozi, Kentse Mpahlwa, Mzwakhe Mbuli, Kuruman Mlanjeni and many others.

To all of you I would like to say: "Be strong like a strong being and keep on coming, I thank you very much."

Contents

Foreword by Spoornet CEO — Zandile Jakavula

It is with a great deal of pleasure and considerable pride that I put pen to paper in order to grace this wonderful gift. There is nothing more exciting than an idea whose time has come. This is an appropriate time for this publication because railways all over the world are re-defining themselves in order to fit in with the global economy. The question that has always flooded my mind is: "Will the organisation of the future repeat the mistakes of the past?" My answer is: "We are bound to repeat the past mistakes if we do not understand that the past is an integral part of the present. It is important to understand the past in order to ameliorate the present and make predictions for the future."

Poetry teaches us about life and the immediate environment. For example, the new employment contract emphasises that everybody is self-employed and that you are paid to add value. The old railways expected the employee to be loyal, hard working, and obedient. Mkiva attempts to demonstrate that these virtues were the hallmark of the successes of the past. The old railways were also characterised by a sense of pride and a sense of belonging. Zolani has thrown down the gauntlet to us all. This calls for railway managers to be "high touch" in this "high tech" environment. Employees are appreciating assets to be treasured and depreciating costs to be developed.

I hope that this book will unite us, until unity is strength and strength becomes power; to build the morale of our people, to build an attitude of mind which will enable us to live and work together harmoniously. The value of Mkiva's work needs no personal testimony from me, his role as Nelson Mandela's praise singer is a memorial more lasting than a personal tribute. His name will go down in the annals of history as a person who introduced industrial poetry as a motivational tool.

May God Almighty coil up warmly to all the people who are going to lay hands on this book. May these poems add value to your life like the psalms of David. For those with the courage to aspire and to believe, railway poetry is motivational. I dedicate myself to the future of railway poetry. At Spoornet we can finally boast that we have our own souvenir to celebrate the new millennium.

From the caboose

Listen, you poets that carol and sing
Stuff about ladies and love and all that,
Can't you get busy with us guys and bring
Some sort of poem from under your hat
Telling how we, though we're common and rough,
Still do our business both early and late?
Here's the refrain you can use in your stuff,
"We are the fellows who bring you the freight."
        Books you are reading,
        Clothes you are needing,
Autos you're speeding at any old rate,
        Pens that you write with,
        Matches you light with –
We are the fellows that bring you the freight!

Sing how we ship you your ham and your eggs
Winter and summer from packer and farm,
Tell how we buck against hoboes and yeggs
Taking our chances of danger and harm;
Toss out a line on the way we must skip
Over a train that is going its gait;
Ice on the top – it's dead easy to slip –
We are the fellows that bring you the freight!
        Stoves that you heat with,
Cards that you cheat with unless you are straight!
        Drinks that you swallow
        And fads that you follow,
We are the fellows that bring you the freight!

Well, Mr. Poet, we've tipped you a hint;
Now you might make us a sort of a song.
Telling the way that we handle our stint
Breaking and switching and jolting along;
Mention that somebody's killed now and then
Doing his duty and meeting his fate,
Make up a song for us railroading men,
We are the fellows who bring you the freight!
        Glasses you peer through,
        Phones that you hear through,
We bring 'em clear through wherever you wait;
        Houses you plot in
        And coffins you rot in –
We are the fellows who bring you the freight!

The Little Karoo

Sudden the desert changes,
The red glare softens and clings,
Till the aching Oudtshoorn ranges,
Stand up like the thrones of kings.

Royal the pageant closes,
Lit by the last of the sun –
Opal and ash-of-roses,
Cinnamon, umber and dun.

We hear the Hottentot herders
As the sheep click past to the fold,
And the crick of the restless girders
As the steel contracts in the cold.

Voices of jackals calling,
And, loud in the hush between,
A morsel of dry earth falling
From the flanks of the scarred ravine.

And the solemn firmament marches,
And the host of heaven rise,
Frames through the iron arches,
Banded and barred by the ties.

Till we feel the far track humming,
And we see her headlight plain,
And we gather and wait her coming –
The wonderful northbound train.

Rudyard Kipling

The builders of the highways

To the builders of the highways that skirt the canyon's brink,
To the men that bind the roadbed fast,
To the men that grade and the men that blast
I raise my glass and drink.
Theirs the great endeavour and the deed of high enterprise;
For they fight their fight with naked hands
'Gainst forest swamps and shifting sands
And the fury of the skies.
To the builders who have fallen, whose graves mark out the line;
To the blind who nevermore may see,
To the maimed and halt in their misery.
In silence drink your wine.
For them no crashing volleys nor roll of muffled drums;
Only the roar of the great rock blast
Is their requiem song when the day is past
And the final darkness comes.
To the engineers, the wizards whose word brooks no delay;
Hearing, the sleeping glens awake,
The snow-plumed hills obeisance make
And lo! The open way.
For them no flaring banners when a bitter fight is won;
No cheering thousands in the street
Their gallant heroes ever greet,
Though dauntless deeds be done.
To the builders of the highways that skirt the canyon's brink,
To the men that bind the roadbed fast,
To the high and low, the first and last,
I raise my glass and drink.

Evelyn Gunn, in the "Canadian Magazine"

The massacre of the innocents, Pretoria

On the Eve of St. Retrenchment, June 30, 1908

There was Mr. Bartleet, always dapper and neat,
A regular dab at accounts,
Though his work was admired, he was first to get fired,
And out of his job he was bounced.
He's gone.

Then on George McClelland the fateful word fell, and
He has to seek further for work,
Re-organisation ne'er thinks of one's station,
But voetsack's you out with a jerk.
He's gone.

Jack Campbell, Paymaster, we thought was a laster
In th' service of Railways S.A.,
But we all got a shock when poor Jack got the knock,
No more will he dish out the pay.
He's gone.

Poor Mr. Sabine, with an air so divine,
And a thirst for his work still unquenched,
Was told with a sniff, "Please take notice forthwith,
You are numbered amongst the retrenched."
He's gone.

And dear Bobby Reid, who hailed from the Tweed,
And Rolling Stock took a delight in,
When retrenched murmured, "Lord, ain't the Railways a fraud,"
With the unemployed now he's a-fighting.
He's gone.

Then Brissenden, smart, with a well-disposed heart,
Took his notice to leave like a Briton,
And right quickly he went with his family to Kent,
(His remarks re. this country can't be written).
He's gone.

Tremewan the teacher, likewise local preacher,
Was next on the list (he made seven),
Said he, "Though we've fears in this sad vale of tears,
There is no retrenchment in Heaven."
He's gone.

Mr. Duggan came next, and said he, "Well, I'm blest,
Retrenchment has made me much wearier,
I've a letter from Dick, so I'll soon cut my stick,
And see Girouard in Nigeria."
He's gone.

Mr. C. Forrest Stroud (of his name he's so proud),
As an actor made quite a big hit,
His last scene was a tall 'un, the curtain has fallen,
And Stroud got his notice to quit.
He's gone.

Percy J. Fallows has made many sorrows,
They told him retrenchment would come,
On the 30th June he went off like a balloon,
And his Railway Service was done.
He's gone.

But cute Sammy Reed he took six months' leave,
And thought he'd be safe from the slaughter,
Out of sight, out of mind, didn't answer this time,
For his notice was sent o'er the water.
He's gone.

Then Armitage thought, as his time here was short,
He'd try prospecting; tools, he would loan 'em,
But 'ere he got back, he'd been given the sack,
"De mortuis nil nisi bonum."
He's gone.

"A Wail from Durban"

By a "Peripathetic" Examiner

The Chief on High he sat him down,
And on his brow there wreathed a frown.
He spake aloud in voice of thunder.
Lo! What he said is writ hereunder.
"These Examining men, what a plague are they,
With naught to do but work and play.
Work and play, the livelong day.
And if perchance they sometimes sleep!
It makes my Chiefly heart to weep.
I'll seek some means that shall be meet,
These men from play and sleep to keep!
I'll teach them all that work is work;
A thing no Service man may shirk!"

So he took a sheet – a fearsome sheet;
He ruled it all with lines so neat;
He squared it o'er; he headed it;
He columned and he numbered it
S.A.42. "Ah! That will do!
These Examining men shall know who's who!"
He sent it out to these men so gay
Who work and play, work and play.
And he told them all, it must be filled,
Or, failing that, they would be pilled.
And the men, poor chaps, they looked askance;
They swore and raved and stamped and danced
And tore their hair and made wry faces
And wished the Chief was sent to blazes.

Said one, "I work twelve hours a day,
And for that work get little pay,
And now atop of all my woes
My chance of sleep forever goes!
S.A.42, it must be filled,
Or else the Chief will have me pilled."
And another man up spake and said,
"I tell the truth; by Mary's head!
For thirteen hours I work on spell,
I get no time off for my meals,
I travel, aye, on tireless wheels;
I have no chance on train, you see,
To fill this form as it should be.
So when at length my spell is o'er,
I sit me down to work yet more.
'Tis three hours' work they've put on me
To fill these forms you here may see.
And if it's right, and if it's well,
That this is Life, then give me Hell!"

A lay of eggs

A worldly wise egg-gearer laid a nest chock full of eggs,
Then rising from her eggery, stood erect upon her pegs.

Eggs-ultantly eggs-claiming as to what she'd been about,
While chanticleer in echo said, "An eggs-cellent lay out."

"A good eggs-ample," Biddy said, "for others' imitation."
"Eggs-actly," chorused all the brood, in one grand cackle-ation.

Then chanticleer broke in again, with shrill "Eggs-cel-si-or,"
In cook-a-doodle lingo, heard a-near and known afar.

And then, again, with flapping wings and air of eggs-altation,
He eggs-ceeded all authority in a sweeping eggs-clamation,

Which these eggs-centric lines, in rhyme, but feebly may express,
Said that his egg eggs-chequer was full to an eggs-cess.

Eggs-citedly eggs-plaining his eggs-traordinary eggs-hibition,
Eggs-plicitly, eggs-ulting and assuring eggs-pedition.

In eggs-tracting from his one eggs-pert an eggs-citing chicken match,
For Biddy, in eggs-pectancy, would eggs-plicate and hatch.

Then they went to "counting chickens," thus one, and two, and three,
One egg, one chick, two eggs, two chicks, as many as may be.

But Farmer Brown in eggs-tasy came across this eggs-tra nest,
And eggs-tradited all the eggs – the reader knows the rest.

A poetic pass

When the late William F. White was traffic manager he received a letter from a man in Kansas, returning an expired annual pass. For some reason another pass had not been sent him. The following verse accompanied the returned pasteboard:

Alas! It is said no more I'll deadhead
My way o'er the glistening rail
Unless Mr. White will consider it right
To send me a pass by the mail.

Mr. White took the expired pass, and wrote several lines across the face, affixing his signature, a complicated series of scratches familiar to every Santa Fe conductor at that time. This is what he wrote:

The conductor will pass this bundle of gas
From March to the middle of Lent;
Like any deadhead without a red
Let him ride to his heart's content.

The pass was accepted unquestioningly by all conductors.
– Exchange.

The quarrelling sisters (Durban and Maritzburg)

"Hullo there, Exchange! Now I want a trunk call;
Be sharp, if you please, or my courage will fall.
I've screwed it up tight, and I mean to talk straight
To the bigoted City that's out of date."

Thus spoke the fair Seaport, one fine winter's day,
To a telephone girl employed in her pay –
The answering ring from the City soon came;
Then both sisters wrangled with might and with main.

A cute little bird somewhere near to Hill Crest,
On the telephone wire was having a rest;
But the heated discussion under his toes
Soon ruffled his plumes and disturbed his repose.

He listened intently to all that was said,
And then to the publisher's office he sped,
And remarked, to the author's absolute bliss,
That the sisters' quarrel went something like this:

"I say, PMB, you've a jolly fine cheek,
To try and attract those who holiday seek,
With dust and your smells they would spend all their wealth
In nursing their bodies again back to health.

"And what can you show them, and where can they go!
They can't get about, for your trams are too slow –
To go near your river is quite sudden death;
And as for a breeze there, you haven't a breath.

"I've heard through the Press that you've just had the nerve
to ask the bluejackets from Durban to swerve,
And have a great gala in your little stream;
Why, your consummate cheek inclines me to scream."

Poor Maritzburg ground her false teeth in her shame,
And tears through her eye-lashes pretty nigh came;
As Durban had openly thrown down the gage,
She answered in accents that quivered with rage:

"You have a swelled head, you low, fish-eating Port,
The cause, I expect, is the fame you have bought
By changing your Beach to a second-hand show;
A place like the Heath, where the masses all go.

"We have a museum full of wonderful sights,
Where scientists spend both their days and their nights.
There's another spot here, I'd like you to mark –
And that is our spacious and beautiful Park.

"We've Parliament here, though quite useless it be;
It rules the whole country from mountains to sea.
Of learning and intellect we are the seat,
And our record of fame takes something to beat."

But Durban just laughed at these wondrous tales,
And asked PMB if she'd caught any whales.
The City retorted with many a sneer
That the smell from the Bluff had poisoned her beer.

'Twas thus that they quarrelled, I'm sorry to say,
And would have continued to this very day;
But the telephone girl chimed in with a sneeze:
"Your three minutes are up – ring off, if you please."

J.S.M.M.

The pride of the C.S.A.R.

You may talk of your Killarney, you may praise your Kyles of Bute,
Or the vineyards of the Rhine, or other scenes of great repute;
You may boast about the Rockies, for scenes both wild and grand,
Or for colour, charm, and sweetness quote Japan's most lovely land.
You may mention any scenery you like, in any clime –
But I have found one little spot to beat it every time.
If you ever come to see it, you'll admit you'd try in vain
To find a spot more lovely than the Shops at Braamfontein.

Ah! the wild weird beauty of the Loco Shed that's there –
And the perfume of the refuse that is lying everywhere!
Where the smoke of locomotives "lighting up" is curling round,
And the paths containing pitfalls for unwary feet abound;
Where the loose iron on the roofing flaps so sadly in the wind,
And employees get bad illnesses of every sort and kind –
And, though young, they grow enfeebled and grey-headed through the strain
Of working in that Paradise, the Shops at Braamfontein!

There, once upon a time, a Loco. Round Shed used to stand,
Till a dynamite explosion moved it to a better land.
In the centre was a turn-table, which to this day is there,
And is our Locomotive Superintendent's special care.
He thinks so highly of it (he has known it now for years)
That when he sees it working he bursts into bitter tears –
Ah, that table, creaking, groaning, like a soul in bitter pain,
It harmonises grandly with the Shops at Braamfontein!

There, in the rainy season, lovely streams and lakes abound,
And life-buoys then are issued out to stop men getting drowned,
Where to go across the yard you have to get into a boat,
And the carpenters stop work, because their benches are afloat;
Where the patient Loco. Foreman wends his weary, watery way,
Expecting all the sheds and shops to fall down any day;
And insurance agents treat an application with disdain –
They won't insure a worker in the Shops at Braamfontein.

There's a thing called a Commission, which has issued a report,
In which they make suggestions of every kind and sort; –
The great thing that they advocate is, "Retrench in every part,"
And, as they were all railway men, they know just where to start.
Now, as the Railway makes a clear two millions every year,
The reason for such drastic measures wasn't very clear.
It puzzled us exceedingly, but now the reason's plain –
They're saving money to re-build the Shops at Braamfontein!

Anon.

Thoughts from the veld

Where does the God of the universe hide? Where does He mantle
His face?
Out where Nirvana and Silence abide, out in the limitless space,
Thrust by the dicta of Science afar, from the world He has fashioned
so well,
Out past the pale of the outermost star – there does the Deity dwell.

Once He was near, very near, to the earth, and His voice was the sigh
of the breeze,
And His were the tones of the wind in its mirth, or the roll and the
roar of the seas.
His was the face in the morning that smiled, His hand dropped the
curtain of night –
But Science spoke out, and a seven-year child prates, "Merely
refraction of light."

Not in the cities of men is He found; there commerce and cant are
enthroned,
Pleasure and luxury riot around, and He and His ways are disòwned.
"Gold" and "Position," Society cries – these are the gods of today;
Bow low at the feet of old Mammon, ye wise, and trample mankind
in your way.

Yet there are some who are sensed of Him, where the fountain
breaks out of the hills,
Where the fern wreath lays hand on the face of the rill, and the
crystal brook tumbles and fills;
Some whom the stars bring a wonderful peace, when the banners of
daylight are furled,
Bidding the throbs of hot passion to cease, and whisp'ring, "All's well
with the world."

Morton H. Wood

An inquiry

Och! Oi'm thinkin's Oi'll be holdin'
An enquoiry of me own,
Into various little matters,
An' some things that should be known;
There are doin's Oi object to,
There are people Oi despoise,
An' the sooner Oi expose them
Will me droopin' spirits roise.

Faix, there's shure to be foine ructions
Whin Oi start oit to enquoire,
An' me foes Oi will be rollin'
In the dust an' in the moir;
Wid confusion they'll be covered,
In addition to the dirt,
An' when loud they howl for cleansin'
Oi'll apply me vitriol squirt.

All the Loco. Men Oi'll froighten,
An' the Maintenance people scare,
Whoile the Traffic men all tremble,
An' upstarts their bristlin' hair;
Thro' the camp Oi'll spread my terror,
Till they go upon their knees,
An' confessin' their transgressions,
Promise iviry thing Oi please.

Faix, wid me no man can troifle,
Oi'm the biggest pot of all,
An' the G.M. quails before me –
Shure, he's at me beck an' call;

So 'tis warnin' Oi'd be givin'
That Oi'm bound to be obeyed,
Which is whoy at my enquoiry
Iviry man an' boy's dismayed.

C.S.A.R.

My harp is hung in silence now

My harp is hung in silence now
Upon the drooping willow's bough;
A stranger in a stranger's land,
In songless solitude I stand.

But oft mine eyes in greedy gaze
Defy the tow'ring mountain's haze,
And, 'spite the desert and the foam,
I dream of thee, and love, and home –

Of sweet embraces fond and long,
And happy hearts, and voice of song,
And friendships, formed in days of yore,
Grown firmer than they were before.

And with the loving and the loved,
Whose faithfulness long years have proved,
'Mid rugged splendour, wild and grand,
I rove my own dear native land.

The woodland stream where first we met,
The quarry-gate where trysts were set,
And many a spot and path I see,
All dear with memories of thee.

'Tis but a dream that will not stay,
A phantom which must glide away,
A meteor's flash, which leaves the night
The darker for its moment's light.

For, while my heart beats wild and high
And gladness glistens in mine eye,
Strange sounds break strangely on my ear,
And I am left a wanderer here.

The babbling of a foreign stream
Mocks all the music of my dream,
And o'er a barren waste I brood
In silent, songless solitude.

Reflections from the Railway Commission Report

(1)
If at close of day or set of sun,
We count the things that we have done,
And, counting, find some self-denying act,
Some word that cheered the heart
Of him who heard, that sent sunshine
Where it went, then we may
Count the day well spent.

(2)
There are none of us so brilliant that we can't learn something new;
There are times when we all must have someone to instruct us what
to do;
We may have lots of knowledge and good common sense to burn;
But bear in mind that all of us have got a lot to learn.

(3)
DON'T GRUNT – DO YOUR STUNT.
There is so much bad in the best of us,
And so much good in the worst of us,
That it hardly behooves any of us,
To talk about the rest of us.

(4)
Ef mebbe in yer system
There's a little sportin' streak,
You'll understand the joy of which
I'm tryin' fur to speak;
When you're kind o' losin' courage
And yer luck is runnin' hard,
And you hold a bob-tail flush, and raise,
And draw a single card

And it ain't the card you wanted –
Well, you don't give in, not yet,
But jes' keep on a raisin'
Till the rest is skeared to bet –
You feel a thrill of pleasure
Sech as comes to very few –
Life's a golden dream of glory
When your bluff goes through.

Letter from Leghorn

Och! Shure, now, Misther Orpington, ye say it is your wish
To tell us all we plase to ask, so plase, now, tell us this.
Now, first of all, a hin will moult her fithers by the score;
But whoi, bedad! – they aren't worn out; they'd last a long time more?
An' thin, bedad! She lays an igg, an', judgin' by the row,
You'd think she'd laid an iliphant; whoi does she do that, now?
My rooshter, now, will crow all day, an' make an awful din,
But – Divil take him – whoi, at night, does he sthrike up agin?
There's some things that you say aren't right;
for instance, now, you said,
Just limewash all the houses out, to kill the flays stone-dead.
Myself it is that's got no house – still, your advice I tried;
I lime-washed all the hins instead, and half the divils doid.
At first I thought I'd send the bill right straight along to you,
But then, I thought, "A railway clerk, shure, doesn't get much screw."
At all events, we'll lave the bill – to make you pay I'd scorn –
But plase to answer phwat I've asked.
Sincerely yours,
Leghorn

Tempus Fugit

Written on receipt of station clock from Stores Department, where it had been sent for repairs, not the old clock on the stair, but the old clock that we stare at:

I'm glad to see your well-known face,
Though it is marred with many a scar;
I'm glad to see you in your place
And hear your tick — you've travelled far.
You've ta'en another lease of life,
They've put your works in good repair,
They've oiled and burnished well each part,
And you will tick for many a year.
You teach us all how time does fly,
And teach us also to prepare
For our last tick – we all must die,
Unknown the hour, or day, or year.

The guard's report

In the year 1890 there was a "perishables" train run in connection with the Early Morning Market from Cape Town to Stellenbosch. It was named the "quiff" train as long as it ran, and was worked by the main line guards. On the return trip from Stellenbosh to Cape Town the under-guard or "strapper", whichever you like to call him, rode on the engine to open the gates at Bosman's Crossing and the 20 mile gate. After the train had passed those gates the guard closed same, and at the 20 mile gate the under-guard returned to the van. On one particular night the driver, fireman and under-guard were having a heated discussion about the different guards who worked the train, and their mode of working, when the engine struck the 20 mile gate. The following was the under-guard's report sent to the Traffic Manager:

"The night was dark and the moon shone bright.
I rode on the engine. We struck the gate
And this is all the information."
Yours truly,
Boy K –

P.S. – The result: Fine 2s. 6d.

The castle builders

"There has been an enormous increase this year in the number of articles left in trains and other public conveyances." – Sunday Chronicle

Our souls are too big for this workaday world
Where toiling and trammelled we groan,
So, weaving romances
And building fine fancies,
Each lives in a world of his own.
The poor little shop-girl is wooed (in her dream)
By the lord of a castle in Spain,
And, lost in a vision
Of rapture Elysian,
She leaves her new boots in the train!

The pound-a-week clerk as he journeys to town
Has wealth and a knighthood in mind,
Surveys his grand marriage,
Then – steps from the carriage
And leaves his umbrella behind.
His opulent master (who travels first class)
Has visions – they're fitful but sweet –
"Life might have been sunny
With love and less money" –
And leaves his kid gloves on the seat!

The stern-visaged spinster of forty-five springs,
Whom no one would venture to kiss,
Sits pensively dreaming
Of lovers' eyes beaming
And lives in a region of bliss;
She dreams, a fair bride, to the altar she's led,
And murmurs, "How happy I am,"
And then – a wild flutter,
"My pound of fresh butter!
I've left it, oh dear, in the tram!"

The world we enjoy is the world of our dreams,
We are greater than life is – alack!
But while we are gilding
The castles we're building
We leave our top coats on the rack.
And while we're in cloudland with beautiful schemes
Our sticks and our parcels are lost
And yet – our romances
And fairylike fancies
I fancy are worth what they cost!

How I saved the Marzipan Express

Recited by H.H. Bodley, the famous comedian

A white-haired man sat listlessly
On a creeper-covered stoep
Before his humble cottage –
When there arose a whoop
From kids that had the Whooping-cough
And a groan from her who had
The gout, and got it chronic,
I couldn't feel but sad.
Within that humble cottage
Were sixteen kids and more
Their father was a pensioner –
Oh dear! Likewise, Oh lor!
That furrowed face, those horny hands
Spoke loud of struggles great,
For eighty years the man had toiled
On the Railways of the State.
"Whence come these white hairs, father?"
I asked in accents low,
When haltingly he made reply –
"Ah well, if you must know,
'Twas on a dark and stormy night
Some fifty years agone,
When the Marzipan Express
From Pans was signalled on.
'Confound the train,' I shouted back,
A man can get no sleep,
For thirty years I've been on nights
It knocks one in a heap
To be disturbed at one a.m.
On each alternate morn,
'Twould break the heart of Morpheus –
The Department's ways I scorn.

They have no thought for working men
When they arrange the trains,
And, when on duty, little time
For 'forty winks' remains.
And so the midnight air was rent
By a whistle loud and shrill,
To the parrot in my dreams.
I shouted – 'At 'im Bill!'
But suddenly I sat up straight:
Gods! The Marzipan Express!
Standing at the signals, too!
Oh Heavens! What a mess!
A "Please explain" I'll get for sure
And p'raps a two bob fine –
See! On the metals something white!
THOSE SIXTEEN KIDS OF MINE!!!
With one strong hand I seized them all
And sent them home to bed,
Then pulled the signal lever
And dropped the blooming red.
The Marzipan Express drew in
As silently I prayed.
Had the driver seen my kids –
Again he'd been delayed.
Its mark the awful strain has left
That night I'll ne'er forget,
From auburn to albino
My lovely locks did get.
I won't forget the night I saved the Marzipan Express."

'Tis hard to bear

'Tis hard to bear unmerited reproof –
To live a life misjudged, misunderstood;
To see our once warm friends now stand aloof,
More credulous of whisper'd ill than good.
'Tis hard when fate environs us with wrong,
And slander spreads, untouch'd by sense of ruth;
'Tis hard when circumstance must tie our tongue,
And those who blame us know but half the truth.
This we must bear, dissembling with the fear
That holds the soul subdued in patient thrall;
And trusting Time to make the darkness clear,
We'll dream of sunshine though the shadows fall.
The Light must shine at last! Be of good cheer,
Our wrongs shall righted be, for God is over all.

The General Manager, M.G.W.R., originally with G. & S.W. Railway

A parting song

We met – 'twas a meeting – our journeys must part;
God speed thee – the greeting went heart into heart,
As one after another his tribute let fall,
But the voice of our brother was sadder than all.
'Twas the hour that must sever our lives' golden chain,
And oh! We might never behold him again.

Hearts that seldom knew sorrow for once felt the sting;
For we knew what the morrow was destined to bring –
Tears to our eyes starting, 'mid silence profound,
As our tokens of parting were handed around.
'Twas the hour that must sever our lives' golden chain,
For oh! We might never behold him again.

Not the short-lived affection grown up in an hour,
Like the rainbow's reflection that shines with the show'r;
Not the butterfly kinship a summer day rears,
Ours was more – 'twas a friendship, the out-come of years.
But the wild waves must sever our lives' golden chain,
And oh! We may never behold him again.

Mr. William Aitkin, G. & S.W. Railway Traffic Inspector

A vote of thanks

"We live in deeds, not years,
In thoughts, not breaths,
In feelings, not in figures on a dial;
We should count time by heart-throbs,
He most lives who thinks most,
Feels the noblest, acts the best."

The lecture was closely followed, and punctuated with marks of appreciation, and a hearty vote of thanks was accorded to Mr. Tatlow by Mr. Chick, who, in thanking Mr. Tatlow for his thoughtful address, expressed the hope that he would again visit Maritzburg, and lecture on the development of the South African Railways.

"Ring in the valiant man, and free,
The larger heart, the kindlier hand;
Ring out the darkness of the land,
Ring in the Christ that is to be."

Steam's triumph

Poem sung by Chas Mackay at the opening of the London and Birmingham Railway

No poetry in railways! Foolish thought
Of a dull brain, to no fine music wrought;
By Mammon dazzled, though the people prize
The gold untold, yet shall not we despise
The triumphs of our time, or fail to see,
Of pregnant mind, the fruitful progeny
Ushering the daylight of the world's new morn?

"Lay down your rails, ye nations near and far;
Yoke your full trains to steam's triumphal car,
Link town to town, and in these iron bands
Unite the strange and oft-embattled lands.
Peace and improvement round each train shall soar,
And knowledge light the ignorance of yore;
Men, joined in amity, shall wonder long
That hate had power to lead their father wrong,
Or that false glory lured their hearts astray,
And made it virtuous and sublime to slay.

"Blessings on science, and her handmaid, steam,
That made Utopia only half a dream,
And showed the fervent of capacious souls,
Who watch the ball of progress as it rolls,
That all as yet completed or begun
Is but the dawning that precedes the sun."

Please to ring the belle

I'll tell you a story that's not in Tom Moore –
Young love likes to knock at a pretty girl's door;
So he call'd upon Lucy – 'twas just 10 o'clock–
Like a spruce *single* man, with a smart *double* knock.

Now, a *hand*-maid, whatever her fingers be at,
Will run like a *puss* when she hears a *rat*-tat;
So Lucy ran up, and in two seconds more
Had *question'd* the stranger and *answer'd* the door.

The *meeting* was bliss, but the *parting* was woe –
For the moment will *come* when such *comers* must *go*;
So she kiss'd him, and whisper'd – poor innocent thing –
"The next time you come, love, pray come with a *ring*".

Tom Hood

To the N.G.R. Magazine

Welcome, thrice told welcome!
A messenger from space;
Dawn of a day on the railed highway,
First in the railway race.

Welcome, thrice told welcome!
The advent of a birth;
On Mercury's wings new life it brings
To the sons of the armoured earth.

Welcome, thrice told welcome!
End of a long drawn night;
Idle dreams and useful themes
Emerge into beauteous light.

Welcome, thrice told welcome!
The news of men's goodwill;
To hard spent lives and the gloom that thrives,
In the round of the mailed mill.

Welcome, thrice told welcome!
Pen wielders of quip and jest;
Let the ship not pause for a tide to cross
The bar of quick success.

Welcome, thrice told welcome!
Then, go ye forth and seek,
Who delve the ground and love the sound
Of the steel and iron shriek.

The song of the flyer

I throw the miles behind me with a never-ending roar;
I pant with heart impetuous for the miles that stretch before;
With ne'er a pause, I leap the tunnel's yawning mouth,
I stop for naught from east to west, for naught from north to south.

The steel blue ribbons glow with pride to bear my passing form;
The signals beckon down the line, through sunlight and in storm;
The mountain lions cower, when they hear my whistle's blast;
The mountain gorges echo as I thunder proudly past.

I hold the road by right of way, a royal race I run,
Nor stay, until my goal is reached, beneath the setting sun.

"Mactat."

A farewell

To Sir David Hunter, K.C.M.G.

Alas! and thou are going vet'ran Chief!
For rigid Statute bids thee leave thy post,
Thy governance tho' long, hath been too brief,
To lose thy service now when needed most,
Thy firm and steadfast mind fulwell hath
These many years her weight of toil borne
Keen mam'ry points the hand of scorn
At those who would thy record soil!
From stage to stage, by careful thought and skill,
Thy System like a noble tree, hath spread
Branches of Commerce o'er each utmost hill
Natalia boasts, and smiling counties led
To fair advantage, gladly honour thee
Who linked them with prosperity.

Then deem not we would have thee so depart,
Without acclaiming here our fond esteem!
No polished phrase wells from the heart,
Nor verbose nothings turbulently teem,
From lips which frame a false conceit
Our panegyric rings a truer chime!
The hours on eagle wings soar sadly fleet,
And hasten on the melancholy time
When thou shall lay thy reins of office down!
Then, we shall miss from thine accustomed place
A friend whose name is clad with fair renown,
Who robes that name of Friend with added grace,
Farewell then Friend whom memory endears,
"Take from our hearts this wish for happy years."

A.E. Kennard

Sir David Hunter

Where rugged mountains rear their heads,
Their forms in purple heather clad,
And rills, with new-born freedom mad,
Go splashing o'er their rocky beds.

Where twilight steals the half of night,
And morn comes early to the grove,
Where feathered songsters sing of love;
There first his eyes beheld the light.

And dear land, while thy sons among,
We think of those still here or gone:
Whom prouder are we all to own
Than he – inspirer of my song.

His landscape was the moor and fell,
Where in the dark, dead days had trod
Brave Covenanters, men of God;
And soon he learned to love them well.

And musing on those martyred men,
Was taught the lesson ne'er forgot,
That earth's best praise is but as naught,
And only Heaven's approval gain.

He chose the strenuous life to lead,
In paths where ran the steel-girt way,
Where effort flags not night nor day,
Obedient to a nation's need.

'Till came the Macedonian call,
"Come o'er and help us or we die."
Responsive to the yearning cry
He came, to bring hope to Natal.

And by the labour of his hand,
And by the brain that knew no rest,
He saw to North, South, East and West,
The gleaming rail embrace the land.

When lean years came, which they do still,
As in Egyptian days, to States –
He sought engagements with the Fates,
And conquered them by strength of will.

Then when the war-like Burghers came,
Bold in their strength as autumn's gale,
The linked battalions of the rail
Which he had taught, gained hones fame.

And while the brave invaders sought
To Britons dare on British soil,
His never-ending care and toil
Attracted even Royal thought.

When railway councils had a call,
Some inter-state compact to trace;
Who at the board a more loved face
Than he, the father of them all.

Thus single-minded, noble-souled,
From duty's path he never swerved;
Beloved by statesmen whom he served,
Revered by all whom he controlled.

Needing no monument to rise
To tell Natal's prosperity;
That he has lived, while they can see,
His noble work with grateful eyes.

But now life's afternoon is come,
And westward slowly glides the sun,
Bringing the rest so nobly won;
And changing toil for ease of home.

And who shall not the wish express,
That for him yet be many a year,
'Midst friends and scenes he loves so dear,
And ever-reigning happiness.

K.C.M.G. General Manager of Railways, Natal

The broken flier

Upon the crap-heap lays the iron horse
Condemned relentlessly, without remorse,
The gallant steed who often drew her load,
Shaming the "sleepers" on the iron road.

Who would have thought that this great ponderous mass,
Shorn of its finery, its polished brass,
Was once the railroad's pride; when in her prime
The fastest "engine" racing in her time.

Her grey old coat once matched obsidian stone!
Was jet black then, with lustre all its own;
Decaying rust has eaten through her side
That "Loco-painter's" art can no more hide.

Her "wheels" are bent, as if some monstrous force
Assisted Time, the all-destroying source,
In breaking up this gallant iron steed
Famous for great endurance, strength, and speed.

Her "buffers" smashed, there is a gaping hole
Right through her "boilers" that contained her soul;
Her "cab" is telescoped, her "smokestack" gone,
Beyond repair, the gallant steed is done.

Her last few years she had been full of wiles;
They could not trust her more than hundred miles;
She got a nasty way of playing pranks
By sticking "check-valve," or by heating "cranks".

She got a knack of blowing off her “steam”,
When it was needed most, she broke a “seam”;
They gave her up at last, in great distract,
When trusty “brake”, for once, refused to act.

She jumped the “rails”, they said, from malice sheer,
Although the “points”, I’m told, “were open clear”;
Right in her way a loaded “ballast train”
(To tell the driver’s fate I will refrain).

Down an embankment then she ploughed her way,
The maddest engine seen for many a day;
At last, exhausted, she fell on her side,
Ending the “flier’s” last most famous ride.

Upon the scrap-heap, now, she found her rest,
Who did her worst yet often did her best;
A broken, helpless, worn-out, sorry steed,
The last remains of a most famous “Reid”.

Ernest Berner

Extract from "McAndrew's Hymn"

"That minds me o' our Viscount loon – Sir Kenneth's kin – the chap
Wi' Russia leather tennis shoon an' spar-decked yachtin' cap.
I showed him round last week, o'er all – an' at the last says he:
"Mister McAndrew, don't you think steam spoils romance at sea?"
Damned ijjit! I'd been doon that morn to see what ailed the throws,
Manholin', on my back – the cranks three inches off my nose.
Romance! Those first-class passengers, they like it very well,
Printed an' bound in little books; but why don't poets tell?
I'm sick of all their quirks an' turns – the loves an' doves they dream –
Lord, send a man like Robbie Burns to sing the song o' steam!
To match wi' Scotia's noblest speech yon orchestra sublime
Whaurto – uplifted like the just – the tail-rods mark the time.
The crank-trows give the double bass, the feed-pump sobs an' heaves,
An' now the main eccentrics start their quarrel on the sheaves:
Her time, her own appointed time, the rocking link-head bides,
Till – hear that note – the rod's return wings glimmerin' through the
guides.
The're all awa'! True beat, full power, the clangin' chorus goes
Clear to the tunnel where they sit, my purring dynamos.
Interdependence absolute, foreseen, ordained, decreed,
To work, ye'll note, at any tilt an' every rate o' speed.
Fra skylight lift to furnace bars, backed, bolted, braced an' stayed,
An' singin' like the mornin' scars for joy that they are made;
While, out o' touch o' vanity, the sweatin thrust-block says:
Not unto us the praise, or man – not unto us the praise!
Now, a'together, hear them lift their lesson – theirs an' mine:
Law, Order, Duty an' Restraint, Obedience, Discipline!
Mill, forge, and try-pit taught them that when rourin' they arose,
An' whiles I wonder if a soul was gi'en them wi' the blows.
Oh for a man to wield it then, in one trip-hammer strain,
Till even first-class passengers could tell the meanin' plain!"

Rudyard Kipling

An engineering joke

I am a junior member of a big society,
And write behind my signature "A, double S, M, E."
I go to all the meetings, and I frequently have spoke,
And sometimes I have ventured on a scientific joke.
And once I made a little pun about a rivet head,
I saw a member eyeing me; when I sat down he said:
"Oh! Bore the main eccentric-strap and fit it on a pin,
And turn the fly-wheel down and fit the governor within,
And bust the blooming cylinder by shrinking on a shank,
And key the valve upon a pipe and clamp it to the crank.
Oh! Wire-draw the piston-rod and throttle till you choke,
But don't ask me to understand an engineering joke!"

"My learned friend," I answered, as I tried to raise a smile,
"I do not comprehend you; is it ignorance or bile
That makes you so excitable? I trust it isn't spleen –
I don't think such a mechanism ever has been seen.
I hope you will forgive me if I add one question more:
Is boring out a cylinder a task you call a bore?" (He answered):
"Oh! Bust the blessed cylinder and clamp it on a crank,
And try the valve upon a pipe and shrink it on a shank,
And bore the main eccentric-strap and fit it on a pin,
And square the fly-wheel up and fit the governor within.
Oh! Wire-draw the piston-rod and use it for a gun!
But don't think I can comprehend a scientific pun."

I remonstrated with him, and I pointed out the fact
That anyone who tried to crank a cylinder was cracked.
I told him 'twas unusual to make a fly-wheel square,
And anyone constructing *one* would never make a *pair.*
When I asked him why a drawer was used in wire-drawing steam,
He started up and gibbered with a maniacal scream:
"Oh! Blow the main eccentric up and use another type,
And turn the fly-wheel down to fit inside the suction pipe,
And bust the wretched cylinder by filling it with oil,
And key the valve into a lock and twist it in a coil,
Oh! Taper the connecting-rod and stuff it in a chest,
But don't ask me to understand so technical a jest."

I'm very seldom nonplussed, but I didn't comprehend,
I wished to hear his history, so went and asked a friend;
He told me 'twas an engineer, a great inventor, who
Had tried to square the circle, and define 'momentum' too –
But someone made a pun on it, which made him lose his wits,
And now he sits around and mopes, and mumbles as he sits:
"Oh! Bust the silly cylinder, by giving it the cramp,
And slap the valve upon its face and use it for a lamp,
And punch the main eccentric-rod and rivet to the flue,
And square the fly-wheel up to do the duty of the screw.
Oh! Wire-draw the piston-rod and stuff it full of grit,
But don't ask me to see the point of scientific wit."

To be merry best becomes you

He would have all as merry
As good company, good wine, good welcome
Can make good people.

I heard the bells on Christmas Day
Their old familiar carols play,
And wild and sweet,
The words repeat,
Of peace on earth, goodwill to men.

Then pealed the bells more loud and deep:
"God is not dead, nor doth He sleep;
The Wrong shall fail,
The Right prevail,
With peace on earth, goodwill to men."

The Stationmaster

Who, from high morn to setting sun
Wrestles with work that ne'er seems done,
Abstracts waybills by the ton,
And drafts press copies,
And in his midnight dreams retains
Memories of naught but books and trains,
Special reports, and "please explains"? –
The Stationmaster.

Who, when returns will not compare,
Stifles the fierce impulse to swear
By offering up a heartfelt prayer
For those who made them;
But when the d——d things still keep wrong,
Warbles a wild, pathetic song,
In accents deep and language strong? –
The Stationmaster.

Who, when some sharp-tongued traveller fly
Jibs at excess, just winks an eye,
Weighs up his boxes, heaves a high,
And sticks him stiffly;
And if that smart man starts to jaw,
Quizzes those boxes o'er and o'er,
Weighs them again, and charges more? –
The Stationmaster.

Who, for whate'er he finds to do,
Seeks no reward but rise of screw,
His three weeks' leave, a suit of blue,
And cheque on pay-day;
And as the years go rolling by,
With oft a tear and oft a sigh,
Looks for a better time on high? –
The Stationmaster

Railway ad.

Breathes there the man, with soul so dead,
Who never to himself hath said:
"My trade of late is getting bad,
I'll try another Railway ad."
If such there be, go mark him well;
For him no bank account shall swell,
No angles watch the golden stair
To welcome home the millionaire.
The man who never asks for trade
By printed line or ad. displayed,
Cares more for rest than worldly gain,
And patronage but gives him pain.
Tread lightly, friends; let no rude sound
Disturb his solitude profound,
Here let him live in calm repose,
Unsought except by men he owes,
And when he dies, go plant him deep,
That naught may break his dreamless sleep;
Where no rude clamour may dispel
The quiet that he loved so well.
And when the world may know its loss,
Place on his grave a wreath of moss,
And on a stone above, "Here lies
A chump who wouldn't advertise."

In memoriam

Dr John Forbes, Railway Medical Officer, Touws River

Gone! Not as a unit from a crowd,
But as the one to whom is owed much,
The minister, the guardian of our health, our friend,
Constant and ever ready.
Self-abnegation all unfeigned
Marked him as one in whom, whoe'er he tended,
Best gifts of mind and heart his ministry attended.
And from the altar of his self-sacrifice arose
The incense of a grateful recognition. At life's close
He left us all his debtors. Not in gold shekel or in pelf,
But debted by the giving of his best, himself.

And should not then his name, with all rich mem'ries fraught
Of man's most noble service to his fellows, be brought
Into high prominence? The niche in which 'tis 'balmed
Be fitting landmark for the guiding of our souls becalmed;
Striving to win, of good, at least a meed.

So be it, and if we to his high plane ascend,
And like him, close our day with labour to the end,
We may unto the prayer of re-uniting (only then)
Respond, and to the prayer acclaim our glad
– Amen.

Kantli von Orthing
Touws River,
17th December, 1911

The man who wins

The man who wins is an average man,
Not built on any peculiar plan:
Not blest with any peculiar luck –
Just steady and earnest and full of pluck.

When asked a question he does not "guess";
He knows, and answers "No" or "Yes";
When set a task that the rest can't do,
He buckles down till he's put it through.

Three things he's learned – that the man who tries
Finds favour in his employer's eyes;
That it pays to know more than one thing well:
That it doesn't pay all he knows to tell.

So he works and waits, till one fine day,
There's a better job with bigger pay;
And then men who shirked whenever they could
Are bossed by the men whose work made good.

For the man who wins is the man who works,
Who neither labour nor trouble shirks;
Who uses his hands, his head, his eyes –
The man who wins is the man who tries.

Traveller: "But don't you find it a bit dull here?"
"Dull, is it? Divil a bit, sorr; sure a reasonable man can find all the height of divershure just sittin' here watchin' the trains go by."
"And how many trains are there a day?"
"Just the wan, sorr."

The Renaming of the Paul Kruger Building: "Umjantshi House"

Great Salutations to Spoornet

A child was born some time ago
Dissocialised and disoriented
Bad mannered and bad natured

Today the child is born again
Today is the rebirth of Spoornet
Ready to be issued with the new birthday certificate
The lotion for motion has been issued

Let us be the thinkers of great thoughts
Let us be the doers of great deeds
Achievement never yet was given
To the people as a gift,
But as a reward bravely earned
Through enormous hard work

We have made distance with the trains
From Mbobela to Loliwe
From Loliwe to Stimela
From Stimela to Songololo
From Songololo to Umjantshi

Come Mafika Mkwanazi and give us
The new name of the child
Come Mafika and tell us the name
Come Mkwanazi and tell us the name

Tell them

Them tell

Tell them that

That them tell

Them that tell

Tell them the new name

ChooChoo_________

Zolani Mkiva